Edge of W

"Elemental. Soul-soothing. Necessary. Victoria's words are a breath of fresh air to the sensitive and weary life traveler. An invitation to step over the edge and face our truest selves, get reacquainted with the disowned pieces of us, and let ourselves fall in love with the wonder within."

—ANDREA BALT, Founder, *Rebelle Society* Creative Rehab, Write Yourself Alive

"Victoria's prose makes the mundane, the to-dos, the realisms of everyday life feel like Sunshine. Her work is like honey-dipping you and allowing you to fall as she catches you on the next line. I've spent hours lost in her work. There isn't such thing as "enough." She encourages the artist to write, the lover to love and for every human on this world to quench their thirst by living."

—JANNE ROBINSON, writer and poet at JanneRobinson.com

"This collection of Victoria Erickson's poetry calls out to readers' souls, past lovers' hearts, the forces of Nature and everything else that has shaped her... to say, 'Come and look at what a kick-ass, amazing world we've got here!' And it's clear, through her eyes and her poems, she is telling the truth... in spades."

—VALERIE GANGAS, Author of
Enlightenment Is Sexy: Every Woman's Guide to a Magical Life

"Victoria writes whispers that are soft yet strong, wanted and needed, confronting but comforting. Her work is like a diary your heart wrote and if strong hugs were words, they would be hers."

—JEREMY GOLDBERG, Founder,
Long Distance Love Bombs

"Victoria has captivated and enchanted our audience at Rebelle Society. An eloquent word-devi, her expression is ecstatically beautiful and describes the natural magic and poetic language of Earth and the human experience."

—TANYA MARKUL, co-founder of *Rebelle Society*, creator of Thug Unicorn By Tanya Markul & YogaWriteNow.org

"Anais Nin said writing was how she managed to "capture the living moments," and our writing our souls out is saving thousands of women on the path. Victoria is one of those wonders whom I can't even recall when we met, or if there was even a time at all when I didn't know her. We share a mutual love of nature's wisdom, poetic thought, and claiming our wildness, refusing to be tamed. She's a bright light for thousands of women walking the awakening path, and where her pen goes, we all follow, finding our own voice."

—SARAH DURHAM WILSON, Founder, Do it Girl,
Author of *DOITGIRL diaries*

"Victoria's words are like soft bookends to the moments of our lives. They hold the moment together with fresh truth, raw honesty and the kind of beauty that comes with opening your eyes, like the first time, every time. With the exasperation of "time flying" by a culture built around speed, her prose reminds and allows us to breathe and be, to notice and to reflect, to source love from the infinite well of our soul and rest in the freedom that lives there—even for just one moment."

—JESSICA DURIVAGE-KERRIDGE, Founder,
Where is My Guru Virtual Center
for Higher Learning

"Victoria Erickson has a gift for evocatively transforming the ordinary into the sheer magic of poetic musing, while bringing to life all the many nuances and shades of feeling. *Edge of Wonder* is full of invigorating reminders to courageously embrace our heartfelt longings, and to never again abandon our deepest passions. This book is alive with daily inspiration!"

—SUSAN FRYBORT, Author of
Hope is a Traveler

"Just below the surface of our everyday thoughts flows a vast ocean of feeling, intuition and awe. Victoria Erickson plumbs these depths like a brave and curious diver; an explorer of the heart. She resurfaces with writing that is an inspiration and a balm. *Edge of Wonder* is a gift. I loved every page."

—LAURA LOWERY, Founder and Editor,
Lucia Journal

Edge of Wonder

Victoria Erickson

ENREALMENT PRESS
TORONTO, CANADA

Published by Enrealment Press
PO Box 64
Acton, Ontario
Canada L7J 2M2

Cover photo by © Aleksandar Borovic – Dreamstime.com
Cover and book design by go-word.com
Printed in the USA

Library and Archives Canada Cataloguing in
Publication

Erickson, Victoria, author
Edge of wonder : notes from the wildness of being /
Victoria Erickson.

Poems.
ISBN 978-0-9947843-1-5 (paperback)
I.Title.

PS3605.R535E44   2015 811'.6   C2015-905977-1

I dedicate this book to all my teachers through the years, my amazingly supportive family, my beautiful grandmother, and to my exceedingly patient publisher and mentor, Jeff Brown.

I also dedicate this book to the ones I've loved, the ones I've lost, and the trials placed throughout my life to spark the burn behind these words.

And to all of you that are on this journey alongside me, learning your edges and allowing your hearts to remain open, so that you too may always remember wonder.

Edge of Wonder

Victoria Erickson

Promise to stay wild with me.
We'll seek and return and stay
and find beauty and the extraordinary
in all the spaces we can claim.
We'll know how to live.
How to breathe magic
into the mundane.

Soulmates aren't the ones
who make you happiest, no.
They're instead the ones
who make you feel the most.
Burning edges and scars and stars.
Old pains and pangs,
captivation and beauty.
Sweetness and madness
and dreamlike surrender.
They hurl you into the abyss.
They taste like hope.

Let your body love what it loves
and what it loves are gentle,
yet powerful things,
same as the way you must
care for it.
Subtle habits and small daily rituals.
Roots and sweet solitude.
The call, connection, and resonance.
Beauty and the elements.
Full-fledged feeling
and wildness
and walking home
and the fiery freedom
to sometimes surrender.

When you spoke,
the light surrounded you,
ribbons of silver and of gold.
Minutes fell off the clock
slipping away and
fading into smooth floors,
through open doors.
A pull drew me to you,
your magnetism.
Two opposite poles.
Like burning sun
and cold rain
to make green things
grow.

Good morning.
I hope you find
today to be
extraordinary.
Are you in love
with the whole
damn world? You
should be. It is
glorious, and I
can't see a
better way to
experience life
than being
madly in love.
With
everything.

It burns sometimes,
staying open,
raw, and real.
With each loss or break
we open wide and wider still.
But the present is so
flawlessly designed
with each lesson,
and difficult test.
It gives back moments
so **vividly stunning**,
the entire sky seems to be
halting the sun, prolonging our time,
and holding in its breath.
There is simply so much beauty.
And so I remain open.

I see you standing there
with a mouthful of poetry
yet a head full of doubt.
You are sharp yet softening
while needing to be split open
and poured out.
So let go.
All the things you now carry
all weights that pull you down
all the beauty you'd forgotten
any flame burned out.
Tell me
what awaits
just beyond
the edge
of your ache.
There's relief
in the speaking.
And there's strength
in being seen.

I have decided that if people were seasons,
some would be summer.
The way they burn as hot
as the sun itself
while seeking quenching truths.
Celestial like the solstice,
always bursting into bloom.
Perhaps I've sensed
a bit of you in me.
A little bit of me in you.

Don't simply brush away
the inexplicable connectedness
we'll occasionally taste
as we experience certain people,
places and works of art.
These mere seconds of quiet synchronicity
and understanding count.
They always count.
You just have to know
and believe it.

Come.
Sit with me now.
We'll gaze at the falling sun
as it grazes this horizon
for I want to talk about
simple nothings
and silent stirrings,
and wild things
with someone
who means everything.

A shattered heart mends
but it has stretched.
The stretching creates room
for even more love.
In fact, the loveliest people
are the ones who've been burnt and broken
and torn at the seams,
yet still send their open hearts
into the world to mend
with love again and again, and again.
You need to feel your life
while you're in it.

I love the silence between two people.
The quiet acknowledgement,
the falling into knowing,
and comfort between words
as we lapse into our own minds,
simply breathing and being
while sharing space and time.
I love the sound of your silences.
I notice them.
I recognize them.
I melt into them.
Because your silences...
your silences sound like mine.

I want to stand with you
on the edge of a mountain,
a valley, or cliff
by the shifting sea.
We can look. We can learn.
We'll take our sweet time
exploring this path,
while unraveling the stories
we cannot yet know,
or see.
Our lives.
This space.
You. Me.

You don't need to choose mediocrity
when fire exists.
Fire is passion
and passion is aliveness,
and for once,
allow your belief
to undo your disbelief
so destiny can hold you
in its ecstatic, flaming grasp.

Leaning into new days
and shifting with each tide,
I'll remember your stillness,
your words,
and your horizons.
And I won't forget
your wild light
that sparked my fire
and furthest dreams
one thousand times,
the match to my flame,
that always burned
deep within
your eyes.

Did you know that it takes a very small time
for ridiculously wonderful things to happen?
That just a few months or weeks
or days or even hours
you could be presented with
an astounding opportunity,
a special person,
a moment you'll never forget,
or perhaps an awakening for the better
that'll shake up everything
you've ever assumed about yourself to be true?

I walk often.
Mornings, evenings,
alone, or with others—
people, dogs,
the scattered shuffling in weeds
beside the road,
or the light in the sky's
current mood.
I'm often asked,
"Where are you going?"
I reply, "Nowhere, really,"
but should be saying, "Everywhere."
When I walk,
I can no longer feel
fear or weight
or worry or pressure,
as they vanish
beneath the rise
of movement,
breath and creative fire.
To me, walking is
recharging my life.

Meditation isn't about
complete, motionless stillness.
It can be found in movement and anywhere.
Find what reignites the flame in you
and go do it often
as that very inward fire is exactly
what will expand, open, and lead you
to everywhere and everything
that's possible in this life.
Forget anything fancy, complicated or expensive
in order to find peace—
simple serenity
to stir the spark
in any way, shape or form
is all you've needed all along.

We gazed upward
at the stars above,
burning and dancing
across the night.
I had words to say
but no way to say them
as I never thought of myself
as quiet, much less silent,
but I was then
because all I could think
was that I wanted to
reach up
and pull down
that violet sky,
like a sparkling, safe light
to wrap around you and I,
where we could forever live
right here
and right now
in this moment,
this midnight,
this dream,
and this paused
paradise.

You keep telling me about moderation.
That a little is enough.
But sometimes for some of us,
a little is not enough.
Because, when it comes to something like
wild walks or vulnerability
or truth or heart-racing conversation
or ecstatic contemplation
or mind-bending intimacy
or all that catapults us into the flow,
form and timelessness
of our own aliveness
I am telling you
that we deserve more than moderation.

When there's a fresh wound in your heart,
keep it open until it heals.
Air it out. Understand it. Dive into it.
Be fierce enough to become it.
If you ignore it, it won't be able to
breathe.
If you ignore it, it will merely deepen,
spread and resurface later,
wanting to release.
And when later happens,
it will hurt even more,
because when later happens,
you won't know what
you're bleeding for.
Remain with it until it clears,
and watch the beauty pour
into your openness.
Remain open to feel lightness.
Remain open to feel free.

It begins in the undercurrents
where it counts.
They want your edges,
your realities, your dreams,
fascinated and captivated,
minds meeting in the center,
where separate worlds collide.
Magnetic magic
only deepening in time.
So promise me
you'll take no one
who shies
from your oceans.
Your tides.

Simplicity will tell you
exactly how it is.
Are there equal parts magic,
contentment and quiet beauty
when you're just being simple?
If not, then wait for it.
Because a good life with someone
is about rediscovering
the beauty of simplicity.

If we stay true to our stories
and exactly who we are
on a deeper level
then the right people
and circumstances
will begin to
effortlessly appear.
There will be a certain pull.
Resonance and familiarity.
There will be connection.
And there will be
more ease.

Keep doing the things
that make you feel something.
Keep doing the things
you're in love with.
And if you don't know what those are just yet,
step out into the world,
and find them.
Because everything
is waiting for you.

If you allow yourself
to only love in halves,
you may find yourself
half clouded, half living,
and eventually perhaps,
half of a person.
Always give
your entire heart, and not only
tiny pieces or jagged missing parts.
Learn to boldly become
the entire sun
and all worthy things
will bloom beneath your fire.

I know you are
tired. Yet—you're
not at all tired
from having
said so much.
You're tired from
not saying all you
still need to say.
There's so much
that needs to seep out
of your skin. To be
held. To be seen. To
be known. And some
words are so strong,
a physical voice
can hardly hold
them. It simply
shakes under their
weight, as they're
released from our
cells, finally freed
from our bones. Keep
showing up for
your own life. Keep
being
courageously true.
To what aches to be
heard in those
silent depths of
you.

There will be certain people
and places that'll open your aliveness,
flooding you with the same awe
and sweet ache
as a thousand daydreams revealed.
Hold these connections close,
for one day you'll know a clear view
of what they truly were
from the beginning—
still moments of perfection
in an ever spinning world.

Forget obstacles,
forget patterns.
Show me your vision of perfection
in an imperfect world.
Tell me what spot
calls to you
while tracing fingers
and eyes
on a softly
spinning globe.
Tell me what's necessary
for your survival,
what's personal,
what's impossible,
what's gigantic,
what's beautiful,
the time you'd had enough
of everything
not being enough,
the last time you didn't want just satisfaction—
you wanted to feel love.
We'll crawl onto balconies
and sit in dark theaters
and watch quiet moons rise
into navy black nights.
We'll become the beat
within the song.
And we'll remember this.
For these lives are swift,
and every moment pulsing.
And precious.

Some people open up
new worlds within us.
Don't always assume
there will be many more to come,
as a great understanding
between two beings is often rare.
Be sure to nurture
and fiercely appreciate
these beautiful friendships
and connections.
You already know who they are.

It's difficult
to tell your story.
To be naked and vulnerable
and raw.
Even when you're naked
from clothing,
you're not truly naked.
You're simply showing skin.
But sometimes
you must be seen
and seen fully
so you can search the eyes
of another
and know that
you're quite okay.
In fact, you're better than okay.
You're gorgeous stardust
and bone and chapters
and light.
You've also been wired
for struggle and imperfection
and overcoming that
and of course this,
and what will eventually come.
And you know what?
You are strong.

I love night conversations best.
Bonds somehow grow deeper in the dark,
our stories climbing
to the surface to be seen.
These are some of the times
that live on longest in our minds—
conversations by candle
or moonlight
with our sleep deprived eyes.

When I speak on the heart,
I'm talking about your creative self,
your internal self,
your intuition,
and your source of power.
Don't be dragged by what
makes the most sense.
Rather, be pulled by what you already know,
and in exactly where it counts: your body.
Stand in the heat of that truth,
because you know what?
It will always be there.
Rather than running from it,
be fierce enough to know it.
Be courageous enough to let it lead you.
Take one small step in that direction. Just one.
Walk slowly if you must.
You'll burn brighter and brighter
as you go.

There are many
different beats
that'll awaken you
from everyday hibernation.
Find the rhythms
in textures,
in elements,
in music,
and movement.
Allow yourself
to be rocked
by connection,
by something greater
than yourself,
by all that propels you
heart-first
into the present
and awaiting world,
for then you'll be moved
even higher
by doing,
by being,
by trusting
your own heat,
burning at the edge
of your most primal desire.
Surrender to the strongest pull
you've known,
and I promise,
it won't lead you astray.
It will bring you home.

We all need space
and reflection.
Like ocean waves,
we must retreat first
before we can build
more strength
in what we're doing.
This reveals itself
in almost all areas of life:
work, love,
friendship, fitness,
flexibility, connection,
creativity.
Trust these natural cycles.

The idea
is to live your life in a way
that makes you feel lit up.
Alive. Excited. Bright.
Half-hearted anything
won't get you there.
It will end up
doing the opposite.

Wherever you are tonight,
go to the window.
Look past the cold air,
any discomforts, or thoughts or tree lines,
or fog and winter winds.
There's a sea of stars above all of it. Let
them open you,
same as they open all our nights,
and remember again and again
that you're in an awesomely wide and wild
universe
that is vast and limitless.
Trust in possibility.
In yourself.
In these words.
In all of this.

Stop saying you don't know.
You already know the truth.
It rests inside your bones
like an anchor.
It whispers when you soften.
It tugs at your weary soul.
Create more confidence to pursue
what's wild.
Light a match.
Stir the flame.
Tie a rope around the dream
that's true.
You see, you've known all along
what you actually want
to do.
You do know.
You will know.
The real you.

Paradise has never been
about places.
It exists in moments.
In connection.
In flashes across time.

As life moves
we need to move with it,
not against it.
Transition happens
whether we're ready or not.
Of course it's difficult
to let go,
to stretch,
to accommodate,
and to be in between here and there yet—
discomfort is inevitable
whether you remain
in a stagnant story
that no longer serves
or you decide
to choose growth.
So choose growth.

I choose love over fear, always.
I'd rather burn in the fire
after touching something true
than not feel anything.

This is your reminder
that you'll consistently deepen.
And it's a lot more fun,
magical, and beautiful
to involve yourself
with only those
who can handle it.
Who will deepen and learn
right alongside you.

Absorb each sensation
and allow it to move through you.
We can recycle what initially
feels like weakness into strength,
ultimately turning grief into empowerment,
like fuel feeds fire or wind
feeds seas and waves.
Remember that every feeling
and emotion is valid, and even necessary,
as we are complicated beings
made of energy, memory,
and immense love,
and were never
meant, nor made
to feel nothing.

Change and growth are painful
not because we're gaining,
but because we're losing.
We lose old ideas.
Old habits. Old stories.
Old comforts.
We shed all that's become
too heavy to carry onward,
wrapped too tight around skin
that needed to finally breathe.
A body that had to break loose
from the once present chapter.
Blank pages had been begging.
Ink aching to write
a new road and world.
A soul that could no longer deny
the taste of something else.
Something that felt true.
Something not yet seen.
We don't have to see something
in order to believe.

If you hesitate
too long on a decision
that both opens
yet frightens you,
the momentum will slow,
and energy will be lost.
You've got to act
when it's there.
You've got to recognize
the surge of "yes"
while it's happening.
Do it now.

When stressed or overwhelmed,
the immediate relief
is always in the softening,
and the surrendering.
Your surrounding world
already offers
its medicine everywhere.
Place your hands in the soil
to feel grounded.
Wade into water
to feel cleansed
and healed.
Fill your lungs
with fresh air
to feel mentally clear.
Raise your face
to the heat of the sun
to feel your own immense power.
You are part of the earth,
and comprised of the very same elements.
And this is something
you should remember.

Wait for someone
who could be the moon for you.
Just as strong,
just as steady,
illuminating changes and seas
and blooming flowers
and summer nights.
They'd wait for you
in the dark.
They'd dance around
the sun.
They'd receive your
primal howls,
your secrets,
your dreams,
and shifting tides.
Wait for the moon.
Wait for nothing less
than what steals
your breath.
What breaks
you open.
What lures
your soul.
What helps
you rise.

On self-care:
Consider every
avenue you take as
a direction closer
to you. Say no
to the good so you
can say yes to the
great. You're
making your way
back into
something both
fulfilling and
true, quietly
reclaiming the
song you then held
so close to your
chest. The song
you once loved, and
knew.

Listen to your gut. The pull.
Don't be afraid.
If you can't stop thinking about it
then you want it, have wanted it,
and will continue to want it.
Dive straight in and ride it out.
The wave will carry you.
Simply trust the water.

I love people
who have been
through adversity and heartache
and obstacles
as impossible
as the sun itself.
They usually make it out
with hearts as warm as gold.
Cores made of fire.
Lives soaked with intention.
Hope like another morning.
They know how to start again—
how to walk through walls
with palms wide open,
and how to begin
at the edge,
and end.
Those to me,
are the best people.

In time,
you'll allow
old pains
to bleed.
Your locks
will break.
You'll find lightness.
And you'll finally
hold the keys.

You should (always)
gaze up at the seas of stars
opening our nights
and remember again and again
that you're in an awesomely
vast and wild universe
where nearly anything
can happen,
and at any given time.
When our perspectives shift,
so do our hearts.

To be fully human
is to be wild.
Wild is the strange pull
and the whispering wisdom.
It's the gentle nudge
and the forceful ache.
It is your truth,
passed down from the ancients,
and the very stream of life
in your blood.
Wild is the soul
where passion and creativity reside,
and the quickening of your heart.
Wild is what is real,
and wild is your home.

We make a home
in the morning air
in which being there together
drawing perceptions
and reflections
from coffee cups
and bare trees
and raw potential
that swirls between
and beneath us
both electric and soft,
charged and gentle
is enough.
Is everything.

What is a night?
A night is shadows,
a night is darkness.
A night is campfires
and candlelit rooms
and silent, rising moons.
A night is
sudden cravings
or habits
that grip you like a fist,
daring you to listen,
to bring them out of hiding,
to be seen,
to be heard,
to be felt,
to be lived.
Breathe in this night
as it reveals
what your days
will never offer,
or give.
Somewhere inside of you
something aches to be heard,
and perhaps by you alone.
The scenery may change.
But not this.

Movement is where this story begins.
The roads are beckoning.
The sun will carry us.
You are a river.
Move to remain fresh,
to stay clear,
and invite what will come
with ease.
Move your body
to feel fluid,
to be open,
to stay primal,
to be free.
Move your mind
so it bursts with ideas
waiting to be birthed,
and move across lands
and roads and waters
to hold the momentum,
to explore,
to grow,
to vibrate,
to breathe.
Beyond this door,
the world awaits.
Take what you can carry.
Movement sharpens
our eyes again,
so we can see.

I'm on a mission to fully inhabit
every felt experience
because how can I touch the world
if I don't touch my own soul?
How can I know light
If I do not know darkness?
How can I hold things safe and steady
with others if I don't feel safe and steady
within myself?

I love when you tell something to someone
and they instantly know what you're talking about
as they've experienced exactly that same thing
or feeling,
and then you have this rapid resonance
and breaking of some barrier
you hadn't realized was in place.
No matter how tiny or unimportant
these exchanges may seem,
we shouldn't forget
that they are mighty.
They soften us.
Like laughter.

There's a certain sensation
when you're meant to belong
in a space.
Like coming home
into the warmth
with a hot mug of something
from the stove
awaiting your lips
beside a bright burning fire
after trudging through a day so cold
you can still feel it
blowing through your insides,
riding the edge
of your crying-for-spring bones.
The space is a comfort,
an exhale, a buzzing,
a sweet memory.
When everything suddenly feels
full of everything.

I sometimes
grow tired of thinking.
Of missing.
The burden of burning.
The weight of planning.
The worry of wondering.
I want to create a moment
from the pull in my chest,
and then another.
I want to trust
in what calls.

I carry veins
that consistently need nature injections
The indoors leave me
distracted and half grasping
for a way to have it again,
lungs aching for air,
feet needing to reground
and eyes always searching for
an open window,
the sun streaming in,
or the closest route
to an inviting door.
Tell me important things
under skies and trees
and I'll soak them in.
I'll remember.

I have such a love/hate relationship with yoga.
I really don't want you.
I need you.
You're painful.
You sweep away the pain.
I'd like a break.
I crave and miss you.
I want to fill my time with other things.
You inspire and ground me for other things.
When you're difficult, you drive me to tears.
When you're good,
you're good beyond words and reason.
You're frustratingly unpredictable.
You continuously show me the root of everything.

I sometimes prefer the swiftness
of all in-betweens.
Autumn, the open road,
gazing out at the sky
out of an airplane window.
The anticipation, the unknown,
the land on the other side,
the momentum,
the magic,
the transition,
and the run before the rise.
Know that the journey
is often more beautiful
than the landing,
as the building of water
is the best part
of the waves, and tides.
Do let the voyage sweetly unfold.
There's no need to rush the destination
as rushing these sort of things
is so sadly overrated.
Carry on. Be with this path.
Explore this space. Flow.

Leaning into new days
and shifting
with each tide,
I'll remember
your stillness,
your words,
and your horizons.
And I won't forget
your wild light
that sparked my fire
and furthest dreams
one thousand times,
the match
to my flame,
that always burned
deep within
your eyes.

Sometimes you must allow your eyes to adjust
to a truer shape of something
you'd once molded
and possibly loved
but perhaps never wanted.
Something to unravel now,
straight from these roots.
Something that at some point,
you loosened your fingers around.
Something that at some stage,
you finally outgrew.
So allow this chapter
to hold you
in darkly wrapped nights
while allowing desires
to just be desires
before lighting that flame
stemmed from your longing
and churned into fuel
so when it is time,
you'll have enough strength
to surrender to fire
that holds the burn long enough
to finally take flight.

Don't mourn memories,
people and moments for long.
You may think
they are gone,
but they have stayed
inside your body.
Stories are the maps
we've drawn,
rolling alongside breath,
strung around our tissue,
pulsing with our heartbeats.

To hold it.
To hold the safety of the slopes,
the sun-drenched heat of a rock,
the play of shadow,
and of light.
How can I take it
with me,
to wrap it around
a belly
that burns for this land
in ways
it cannot escape,
like a soft animal
slipping away
into the night,
or the fiery ball
that is the sun
existing as only an echo
of faded hues
now fallen into twilight?
I don't want to leave
with only the ghost
of this place.
I want the heat
that fuels
the wild growth
and the ground
as steady
from where
I stand
to hold me

as it does
these trees,
rocking me calm
and rooted,
while locking this
fleeting feeling
safe.

There are certain landscapes and places
that call to us again and again.
There isn't always a reason,
rationalization or rhythm to this—
it's just the way of things.
Some of us may prefer the ocean and its tides,
some the desert—barren and serene,
some of us the eastern forests of vibrant green,
and some, the mountains, grand, wild, and sweeping.
When you think of the land you inhabit,
is it the one that calls you home?
Is it the one that comforts your body
and being down to the bones?
When you close your eyes,
what scenery do you most long for?
Remember, that we're able to derive
great strength and energy
from our surroundings
when they're right for us.
Live in your strength.

We fill our cups with so much,
we must find days to empty out.
It's okay to love your silences
without distress when it's time
to listen to your own soft stillness.
Submit to serenity often.
Allow calmness to claim you.

Somewhere close
yet far enough,
there's a place
where time cannot reach.
A place suspended
in a moment,
where the earth
stops turning
and where you know
I'll be waiting.
I'll be the wings
that keep your heart
in the clouds
and you'll be the anchor
that keeps my feet
on the ground.

People are like continents.
It sometimes takes more than a lifetime
to explore the trails,
mysteries and lands
in a single human being.
And there will be storms together,
darker than you've ever seen,
shaking two fragile hearts
like raging rain
to scattered sands
and wild winds
to lonely trees.
And there will be days
when you simply want to run,
to another land across a sweeping sea,
under an entirely different burning sun.
But here's the thing about the continents we love,
down to our tired bones:
we know the one that calls us back
to unpack our luggage.
We always know which one
is truly home.

I don't desire mediocre anything.
I crave the beauty and belly
of the extraordinary,
I want to burn
at the right temperature.
I want to feel
my own heartbeat.

Sure. I'll make
small talk. Chit
chat.
Discuss the ins and
outs of a "typical"
day.
Pass the time
lightly. Say tiny
things. I'm happy
to tread surfaces
with a smile,
and will.
Sometimes.
Yet—when I look at
you,
I know there are
layers.
Dimensions.
Collections of
ancient wisdom.
Roads. Stories on
stories on stories.
Core needs.
Humanness.
This is where I
light up.
This is where I
thrive.
You can't be caged
in a pool for long.
Not when you're
someone
who wants oceans.

I hear so many people
talk about finishing chores
and wanting a calm mind
and meditative environment
before they sit down
to try and write.
Not me.
I need anxiety.
Grit. Intensity.
Energy.
I want to feel like a hurricane
about to rock the darn ocean
before emptying out
spiraling, twisting rain all over the page.
I won't write unless it grips
and pulls at me,
demanding me to drop
all else until it's done.
I've pulled over into parking lots with my
phone.
Stood against buildings with a notebook.
Ducked away from crowds with paper.
If you don't feel the words coming,
ready to physically explode
out of your own raw experience,
walk away.
Walk away
until you're ready.

Tell me.
What did your eyes do
before they sensed
the frightening edge
of your own destiny
slowly rising into view?

We are paradoxes.
Made of both steel
and fragile feathers.
Rooted yet with wings.
Our imagination both gifts us the world
and exiles us from it.
We may want both
shimmering silver cities
and quiet, serene trees.
We want this, now.
And we want soaring, slippery,
taunting dreams.
We want them close.
We also want to be free.
It doesn't matter darling.
Accept all of your turns.
Your twists.
Your shifting seas.
Despite all of this,
you are still flawless.
Unshakable.
Human after all.

I see you standing there,
straining to remain meticulous
while your heart strains
against the cramped cage
that contains it.

And you were the sun for me.
The rising and falling
and rising again.
The brightening.
The enormity.
The brilliance.
The wakening.
The burning.
The scorching.
The missing.

When you reach your edge, soften.
Soften until you slip through
the constraints
and can create
a new rhythm,
a new route,
a new release.
Water is soft yet powerful.
Reach your edge,
and soften.

Tonight, you may
be sorrowful or
silent, empty or
alone, but you
have the moon, and
you have your
breath, and in
inhaling the
wonder of these
alone, you might
find yourself
wrapped in the soft
shawl of gentle
relief that this
very moment is
beautiful, and more
than worthy of
perfect love.

Every day,
I'm surrounded by people
too caught inside their own minds,
trapped between their edges and scowls,
sucked in a whirlwind of themselves,
believing they're the center.
That the planet revolves around one.
But I can tell you are different.
I know you can sense
that there's more than your flame.
I know you can feel the sun.

If the world is
patiently waiting
for everyone else's
senses to grow
sharper to reveal
magical things,
all you need to do
is step outside and
ride the energy of
the earth, for
there's always a
brilliant sunrise,
rolling fog,
shifting seasons,
and rising waters
to experience, as
well as new,
inviting lands to
step foot on.

And the view is
glorious.

Tell me about
how as a child,
you allowed
colors to come
like water takes in
the falling sun.
How they'd seep into
your wakeful mind,
their beauty
drowning uncertainties,
your hidden tears
wiped dry.
This is the rhythm
you can still reach for,
and find.
This is the dream
and the remembering
that the ocean
still touches
the sky.

Perfectionism is merely
an endless treadmill
of self-destruction
that'll only build momentum
until you're running at unsustainable speeds.
Rather than remaining a slave to the illusions
you perceive as safe,
step off the treadmill
and live as the piece of art you are:
messy, colorful, fluid, and adaptable to change,
mistakes, shifts, surprises, pain, and of course,
immeasurable moments of beauty.
It's only outside the self-imposed walls
of perfect self-imprisonment
that you'll finally touch
the true meaning of freedom.

When it comes to creation
you must begin from below the belly
and through the spine.
The internal stirrings.
Where it aches. Where it sighs.
You must reach into that prana,
where it pulses through the heart,
pull that energy upward,
and pour it all out.
If you begin in the head
and analyze what to say or do,
it won't seep into other people.
They won't feel it where it counts
unless it comes straight from the depths,
and vulnerability of you.

I'd like to know about
these forest paths.
Their bending,
their breaking,
their changes,
their seasons.
How we'll step into our own,
learning to protect
each other's breathing,
learning to breathe together,
to share space,
to give space,
to become
the very trees themselves,
steady in our wild growth
our roots deeper
than the ground itself
and strength sometimes
stronger than reason.

Maybe we could
stop time for a few days
without falling far behind.
Maybe we could
jump in the car
somewhere beautiful
and remote.
We'll shed our pain and armor,
turn on the music,
and explore these places,
these towns,
and these dreams.
Yours and mine.
We'll just ride it
all out for awhile.
We'll just drive.

I've never known a person
who tries to control
anyone or everything
to be happy or content.
Micro-managing, labeling,
perfectionism, and strict expectations
should be sent away
in the tiny boxes
they place and trap people in
when overcome by them.
We arrive into this world as energy,
same as stars, wildlife,
wind and ocean.
Messy, raw,
and continuously perfect
in our chaos.
Release the need to control,
and instead surrender
to your own natural rhythm,
as expansive, accepting and open
to new circumstances and situations
as air itself.
That is how you'll flow.
That is how you'll thrive.

The tough questions:
Is it a wholehearted yes or a sometimes?
Does it simply feel "right"
or strained and constrictive?
Natural and worth doing
or an effort too tiring to make?
Magnetic or repelling?
Inspiring or draining?
Use flow instead of force
or else it's simply not for you.
Gracefully back away
and shift toward what IS for you.
Right here. Right now.
What or whom excites you,
reassures you,
and brings you alive?
Because life is never not now.

I meant to tell you
the moon is still silver.
It still rises same as it used to rise,
shedding light onto cities and lands
softened by the coming of night.

I meant to tell you that I still gaze up,
same as when you were here,
and that in the stillest of hours
while carrying a heart
as wide as the sea,
if I soak in that moon,
it may bring some relief.

I meant to tell you that
I still taste your song in me.
It comes in waves
under silent skies,
It threatens my sanity.

How you came and you went
long before I could tell you
I didn't want you
to leave.

But you did.
And the moon is still silver.

So here I stand
left with echos
of us

And those nights
that used
to breathe.

If I had two weeks,
I'd take you to places
that make the soul
a little less thirsty—
places that'll hold us in their hills
as the sun blankets the lands
with hopeful orange light.
We'd soften gently with dusk,
knowing that time will take care of us,
because when you believe in time,
then time will believe in you and I.

You made yourself
from the earth,
the meadows,
the ground below us,
holding this planet steady.
I made myself
from the lightning and rain,
hovering above your quiet grounds
'til I am called
when your solid lands
are thirsty, and ready.
Meanwhile, the earth spins on.
Meanwhile, the wind grows strength
in shedding truths and whispers
of silent knowing.
Just as soil feeds the world,
and water feeds the soil,
we were not made to exist
in this world without another's voice on the line,
or strong hand in the dark.
We are here to support one another,
by growing separately,
yet still always together.
To light each other's spark.

As time treads on,
we may think memories become muddled and vague,
slowly disappearing with each year, but this
isn't the case.
The body remembers.
Because when you revisit a place
it has a way of pulling the past up
from the depths of your bones
flooding your bloodstream
with old familiar feelings,
only this time they're more concentrated,
more potent, and more clear.
Like a time machine.
A time machine of remembrance and longing;
longing to hold on, longing to go back,
longing to never forget again.
But nothing is ever truly forgotten,
just stored inside us like a series of faded
snapshots,
simply waiting for recognition
to form the full picture.
I used to journal to keep track of time,
afraid I would lose too many moments
if they weren't permanently pressed to a page in
black ink.
But now I realize that all we really need
are quiet reminders.
Because the memories...
the memories always remain.

I think everyone should encourage everyone.
We have enough self-created walls
and people who unknowingly
also build them into our psyches,
simply by discouraging us.
Encouragers build doors
instead of walls just by believing.

We spend so much time in our heads.
We become slaves to visions of the future
or drained by past memories,
or pulled into technology
multiple times within a single hour.
I often feel guilty
that I don't allow myself
the full blown sensory experience
every moment deserves.
To be present might be exactly
what we've needed all along.
To feel a place while we're in it.
To be fully with people
while sharing time.
To know this moment
and this moment only
may actually be the closest thing
to ecstatic living we'll experience.
So wherever you are, be there.
In your body. One foot in front of the next.

Sensitive types and creativity
go hand and hand,
because their rawness and innate ability
to pick up on information and energy
that others don't feel
can easily be translated
into art and passionate expression.
So rescue that fleetingly gorgeous moment,
then recycle it through your chosen medium.
Perhaps you can make your guitar cry,
or weave beautiful cloth into wearable clothing
or drip powerful words like blood on a page,
or capture that perfect light with your camera
before you.
Just create, create, then create some more
so other people can see through your eyes,
sensitive person.

If there's no hope in your view
we'll create a new view
and drape it
with sunlight and breeze
and soft green hills
to shield us
from tough unknowns.
Believe with me as I'm tired
of those that don't
and would like to live
with a heart full of summer
and a headful
of hope.

There are worlds within this world
where you will thrive.
Find them.
Flip "too good to be true" into,
"this is good, and true."

When we listen to certain types of music
or soak our eyes with paintings
or fill our lungs with poems,
it all begins to blend
and run through us,
quietly becoming part of our blood,
flesh and bones.
We always carry
the art we've loved.

I crave the ones
who've seen
confusion and
known struggle,
who have pulled
themselves up from
the shackles of
heartache and
strife,
disappointment
and darkness,
exhaustion and
drain and have
risen with a heart
as open and
unwaveringly wide
as the ocean itself.
Give me those
people. The brave.
the vulnerable, the
wise, the ones who
care for a world,
and how to better
it along with
themselves. To
know their ability
in making waves,
in shifting
patterns with tides
and in creating
change. Let us
become that open
ocean. And make it
rise.

Life is passing
rapidly. Fiercely
commit to every
moment you find
beautiful and
remember it. Record
it. Fully, whole-
heartedly inhabit
it. Awareness is one
of the greatest
things you can
possess in this life
as it is as
important as the
very air we breathe
and water we drink
to stay alive.

I am curious and I
am careful.
I dance around the
edges of you
like dusk to towns
before draping
the shapes and
lines.
I don't know what
it's called—
the space before
hands collide,
but it fills my
lungs
the way one aches
for
water and warmth
and air,
or same as the way
our bones need rest
wishing to slow
the spinning
earth,
to halt the passage
of time.

I think I'm a
lover of fire.
Candles and
incense,
bonfires and
fireplaces,
passion and
creative force,
stars and sage,
the rising and
falling of the
sun. The
destruction of
the old, the
birth of the
new.
Igniting the
flame. Being set
ablaze. The
heat. The
energy.
The burn.

Time is running
forth like a train
blowing through
another town and
day, whirling
through exits,
hallways,
doorways. Stand up.
Walk toward a
window. Open your
eyes and let the
sky in. I know
you're thirsty.

Dwelling on the negative merely lowers your vibration and creates sickness in the mind and body. Use your internal strength and willpower to rise above the thoughts pulling you down and watch your world rise alongside you, continuing to meet you exactly where you are.

Listen to the
night as the night
knows your truths,
your stories, your
aches, your dreams,
your cravings,
your forgotten
memories, not so
forgotten.

Aliveness is the
energy behind
everything we do
whether we're
expressing
through movement,
acting from love,
or touching the earth, the
community, the
greater good, and
ultimately, the
world itself.
Nurture this.

People fascinate
me. Their bodies,
their brains, their
emotions, their
ideals, their
histories, their
choices, and their
dreams. Their
stories. It all
comes back to
stories.
Everything
everywhere is
ultimately a
story.

We didn't talk
about much at
all, yet I felt
myself soaring
from your
sleep-soaked
voice as though
soon you'd be
holding my
hand instead of
simply on the
line, while
sending an
electric
current down
my spine in
such a way I
could possibly
implode with
something so
more than
myself, for it
was astounding
that the light
touch of a
person's skin
could do this to
mine.
We were dancing
underneath the
sun, and I was
once again
nineteen.

As I watched my mom decorate her tree last night,
I was thinking that "home" is
never a specific town or house or room
where the tree resides.
It's instead a series of moments we gather—
like snapshots on a string,
of the times spent with people we love most.
The quietest moments that pause the longest
and echo the loudest in a quickly turning world.
If you could collect one crucial thing in this life,
let it be the moments, the snapshots,
the collection of still points that make up "home",
and hold them close in spaces
that remain open when you need to return.

I've always
wondered
Why the words we
form
Can never match
what's behind them.
But when our eyes
meet and lock
Emotions rush
through my veins
Intoxicating my
brain
Melting words into
silence
Flung as wide as a
sea
I would dive in and
swim through
Just so I can get
across
To wrap these arms,
This world
These words
Without words
Around you.

Gazing upward at the night sky is the closest feeling we have to time travel. Suddenly you're 8 again, camping in the summer. You're 13, leaving a movie theater with friends. You're 22 on a city hill, gazing at the skies above bright urban lights, squinting so they meet in the middle, where everything blurs and sweetly collides. You're suddenly everyone you've been, everyone you will be. Want to be. Already are. Infinite.

A list of random
and unrelated
things to remember:

—Time heals.
—Mountain winds
sound exactly like
ocean waves.
—You are worth
everything now.
—Walls can be
destroyed.
—The sun always
rises (and is
always beautiful).
—Children know the
answers.
—There is music in
everything.
—Logic doesn't
produce magic.
—Somewhere,
somebody loves
you.
—You don't need to
choose mediocre
when fire exists.
—The moon
orchestrates our
nights and tides.
—Trees can grow

through rock.
-Your heart
expands when it's
broken.
-You should do it
now.

I'm tired of long-
term goals and
rules. I want to set
intentions instead,
breathing and
existing in this
moment every step
of the way. I've
always written
from my body
rather than my
head, and that's
exactly how I want
to make my
decisions: not from
logic or emotion
but from my very
core itself. That's
where the real
power lies, and also
how we begin to
free ourselves.

You can be in love
with one thousand
views and skylines
and souls and
minds at once.
Don't apologize for
your burn, your
passion, or your
enthusiasm.
Enthusiasm
propels the world.

We wanted to be
the sky,
swallowing the
sun while arm
in arm and
loose in the
open
landscapes,
radiating
outward and
spreading
light into the
furthest
corners of an
aching world.

When we nourish
ourselves with
good people,
projects,
surroundings,
scenery, love,
magic, beauty and
self-care, we
radiate light into
the world and
continually
sharpen our
vision, perception,
and clarity all at
once. This in turn
spreads to other
beings which
spreads to even
more. Remember
that one tiny drop
can raise an ocean.
Keep wanting.
Desiring. Doing.
Breathing in the
sweet things.

Going to bed in
awe of everything.
Open windows.
Another night
carrying the
sounds of thick
trees and crickets
and distant coyote
howls. Restlessness
looms and distracts
and dares us before
we're ready. The
stars burn above.
Summer is close.
Life is so wild and
difficult and
amazingly
enchanting.

Basically this means if you are sensitive, you have the ability to see colors and feel energy the way others hear jet planes. The world takes on a rich tapestry of immense gorgeousness at almost every turn, which then fuels your imagination and makes you spin with aliveness. And aliveness is a grand thing.

Then I said
goodnight and
tucked you away
inside a place
called Nostalgia,
where you'll
always remain
unspoiled,
somewhere between
my lungs that used
to breathe ocean
air, and my belly
that fluttered with
hope.

Let's not travel to
tick things off
lists
or collect half
hearted semi
treasures
to be placed in
dusty drawers in
empty rooms.
Rather, we'll
travel to find
grounds and
rooftops
and tiny hidden
parks,
where we'll sit and
dismiss the
passing time,
spun in the city's
web 'til we've
surrendered,
content to be spent
and consumed.
I need to feel a
place while I'm in
it.

Once you reunite
with your clarity,
let it lubricate
your parched soul,
be the wave you
want to glide on
and the energy you
give your body to.
Allow it be the
friend you become
powerfully
fearless with and
the very medicine
you need to
dissolve your
empty parts. Let it
halt your restless
yearning and lead
your beautiful
heart.

There's always a
few moments at
dusk when the sky
sheds purple and
the world seems to
exhale out the day.
I'm learning to
breathe alongside
it. I'm learning to
soften into the in-
betweens, to be
content with the
not knowing, to
innately
understand when
it's fine to stop
all of the reaching
for a bit and just
be and believe.

Road trips are
the equivalent
of human wings.
Ask me to go on
one, anywhere.
We'll stop in
every small
town and learn
the history and
stories, feel the
ground and
capture the
spirit. Then
we'll turn it
into our own
story that will
live inside our
history to
carry with us,
always. Because
stories are more
important than
things.

There are certain
people that'll
inhabit a small,
quiet space inside
your heart despite
any circumstance,
happening, or
situation. They
left a piece of
themselves when
your souls
collided upon
impact. And there
they'll always
subtly remain.

Your story isn't
calm. The road has
been chaotic at
times, filled with
detours and rain
and loss so sudden,
and soon. Sometimes
the bliss was so
elevated your
heart could hardly
hold it. Sometimes
it was maddening
to have, and then
to lose. You learn
soon enough that
it hardly ever goes
as planned—
gentle, easy, and
smooth. But that
my friend, is what
makes you
fascinating. You
have something
to tell. Something
you've walked
through.
Something wild.
Something
courageous.
Something true.
You're made of
stories within
stories within even
more stories. Those
quiet depths of
you.

How can you hold
things safe and
steady with others
if you don't hold
things safe and
steady within
yourself? How can
you swim deep into
a soul when you
can't grasp or
ignite your own?
This is why we do
the work to become.
Because, love.
Because none of us
are truly happy
with shallow
existences. But
without first
knowing ourselves,
we'll get trapped
in tiny ponds.
When all we ever
longed for was the
ocean, all along.

When there's a
fresh wound in
your heart, keep it
open until it
heals. Air it out.
Understand it. Dive
into it. Be fierce
enough to become
it. If you ignore
it, it won't be able
to breathe. If you
ignore it, it will
merely deepen,
spread and
resurface later,
wanting to release.
And when later
happens, it will
hurt even more,
because when later
happens, you won't
know what you're
bleeding for.
Remain with it
until it clears,
and watch the
beauty pour into
your openness.
Remain open to feel
lightness. Remain
open to feel free.

Like most
sensitive souls
you already
know you're
sensitive.
You soak up
others moods
and desires like
a sponge. You
absorb
sensation the
way a
paintbrush
grasps each
color it touches
on a palette.
The ethereal
beauty of a
dandelion, the
shift of a
season, the
climax of a
song, or a
certain
stirring scent
can awaken
such wonder
they'll become
your very
breath itself—
moving
through you as
fuel does to fire
and wind does
to waves.

Women are
powerful, and I see
them stifle this
every. single. day.
Stop looking to be
saved and hiding
your magic. Stop
tossing aside your
voice and valid
emotions. Stop
wasting your time
with fake friends
and chasing men
like they're cures.
Material things,
better jobs, and
other people—they
won't fill your
gap. Only you can
do that. Life is
short. Rise up and
step back into
your awesome,
innate power. You
are compassion and
creative force and
divine life itself.
You are a Goddess.

Life is too short
for pretend. Don't
do things by
halves as casual is
casualty, and
time isn't
renewable. Go
deeper. Live with
integrity and
unwavering
intention. Choose
real.

Often times, a
person will think
they know you by
piecing together
tiny facts and
arranging those
pieces into a
puzzle that makes
sense to them. If we
don't know
ourselves very
well, we'll
mistakenly believe
them, and drift
toward where they
tell us to swim,
only to drown in
our own confusion.

Here's the truth:
it's important to
take the necessary
steps to find out
who you are.
Because you hold
endless depths
below the surface
of a few facts and
pieces and past
decisions. You
aren't only the
ripples others can
see. You are made of
oceans.

Meaning and
purpose don't come
in the forms of
great
accomplishments or
undertakings.
Rather, they reveal
themselves on some
randomly idle
weekday morning
when you realize
how much you love
someone or that
you're doing all
you can with what
you can carry in
the place you are
with the time you
have with what you
care about.

Take me unprepared
to your towns, your visions,
your imperfections,
your views, your trees.
Carve a quiet canyon
inside my chest
so I can hear you beat
so I can feel you breathe.
Unknown and known,
we'll each
be moved
outside of the space
of these common,
everyday things.
And if only for a moment
rediscover what it means
to feel shatteringly alive.
To remember
that we are free.

I wanted to ask
you about your
vision of
perfection in an
imperfect world, or
what side of the
earth calls out to
you when you
touch a physical
globe, or maybe
about your
greatest heartache
and how you still
go on as your
world continues
turning, or what
you do with a
memory once lodged
inside your bones
that's still
breathing, and
burning.

But you're still a
stranger, and I'm
overly polite, so
I'll ask all about
your day when I'd
rather know about
your life.

Half of me is
filled with
bursting words and
half of me is
painfully shy. I
crave solitude yet
also crave people. I
want to pour life
and love into
everything yet
also nurture my
self-care and go
gently. I want to
live within the
rush of primal,
intuitive decision,
yet also wish to
sit and
contemplate. This
is the messiness of
life- that we all
carry multitudes,
so must sit with
the shifts. We are
complicated
creatures, and the
balance comes from
that
understanding. Be
okay with the flow.
Be water. Flexible

and soft. Subtly
powerful and open.
Wild and serene.
Able to carry and
accept all changes,
yet still led by
the pull of steady
tides. It is
enough.

Perfect is empty.
Boring. Vapid.
Exhausting.

Be interesting. Be
interested. Be
anything except
on a quest for
perfect.

Forests will
always hold your
secrets, for that's
what forests are
for. To separate and
hide things. To
protect, to comfort,
to hold, to envelop,
to demonstrate, to
slow down, to hold,
to teach. Go to the
trees to explore
your questions and
dreams. Go to the
trees to desire and
seek. The world
will listen as you
walk, watch, soften
and breathe.

We arrive into
this world as
energy, same as
stars, wildlife,
wind and ocean.
Messy, raw, and
continuously
perfect in our
chaos. Release the
need to control,
and instead
surrender to your
own natural
rhythm, as
expansive,
accepting and open
to new
circumstances and
situations as air
itself. That is how
you'll thrive.

We're all drawn to
different places,
and I've always
been mountain
girl. I think of
them all day, and
sometimes ask
myself if it's a
little less
dangerous and
perhaps more
sustainable to find
absolute ecstatic
bliss by falling
madly in love with
landscapes rather
than people as it's
also immensely
grounding in
every sense of the
word? I want to
explore them, sleep
inside the heat and
cold of them,
experience all
their seasons,
share their
crooked, winding,
wild paths, and
grow with them
alongside me.
They've always felt
like gorgeous
undeniable
mystery and home
all at once. The
mountains.

If you ever find
yourself empty
from something
you cannot know or
name, find a
stretch of ocean, a
field, or
mountainside, or
even clouds, or
trees. Because there
are 1,000 simple
ways to fill your
tired soul so you
can remember how
to be, how to see,
and most
importantly, how
to breathe.

My advice to you
is to soften into
the discomfort.
Accept it. Know
that it's gifting
you growth, fuel,
and grit. Whatever
it may be that
you're claiming
this year as your
desire and dream, I
wish you the
comfort within the
discomfort. The
stillness within
the unease. The
softening within
the stretch. And
mostly, I wish you
the match that
lights and revives
the fire to keep
you going. Because
you can. Keep
going.

An artist is
typically a
being that is
filled with so
much passion,
love, or pain
for certain
lands, people,
ideas, or images
that all they
can do with
that overflow
is bleed it out
by creating.
And with this
type of art, the
energy will be
shifted from the
depths of them
and into the
depths of the
audience to be
felt. It is a
dance. A
transference.
An intimacy. It
is to touch and
awaken another
human in a
place they
hadn't known

was aching, or
sleeping. Both
are opened.
Both are
nourished. Both
are
transformed.

Refuse to be that
person that, like
so many others is
still driving down
the same road,
years down the
line, mournfully
longing to go back
in time to be given
just one more
chance to take the
road that they
know they should
have taken because
they dismissed all
possible,
extraordinary
signs. It'll never
get easier to make
the leap and this
is your chance; so
make the change.
Take the road now.

Right now, I urge
you to unravel the
listless, rigid
parts and feed your
wild, because it is
the wild you, not
the barely alive,
embedded-into-
routine, zombie-
like you that is
now struggling for
air. For turn on.
For sweet prana.
Restore the wild
and the warrior.

You shouldn't have
to get sick or halt
domesticity to find
it; you just need to
remember that you
are human, still
very much alive,
and wickedly,
wildly
extraordinary.

Everyday poetry:
the collision of
breath and winter,
the pause between
daylight and dusk,
the breakthrough
in the body, the
sweet spot in the
song, the photos in
the attic, the
rediscovery of a
note, the strokes of
paint on canvas,
the silence in the
nights, and the
space after letting
go.

A heart full of
maps. Hope like an
ocean.

About the Author

Victoria Erickson is a grounded idealist who's been writing the world awake since she was a child. Forever embodied and heart driven, she believes deeply in innate wildness, intuitive body intelligence, and in harnessing the power of sensitivity. A wildly popular columnist with *Rebelle Society*, *Edge of Wonder* is her first collection of inspired writings. You can connect with Victoria's work at www.facebook.com/VictoriaEricksonwriter.